ACTIVITY BOOK

macmillan education

Carol Read • Mark Ormerod

Welcome to the Tiger Tracks Social Learning Network

Lesson 1

1 Look and write the countries.

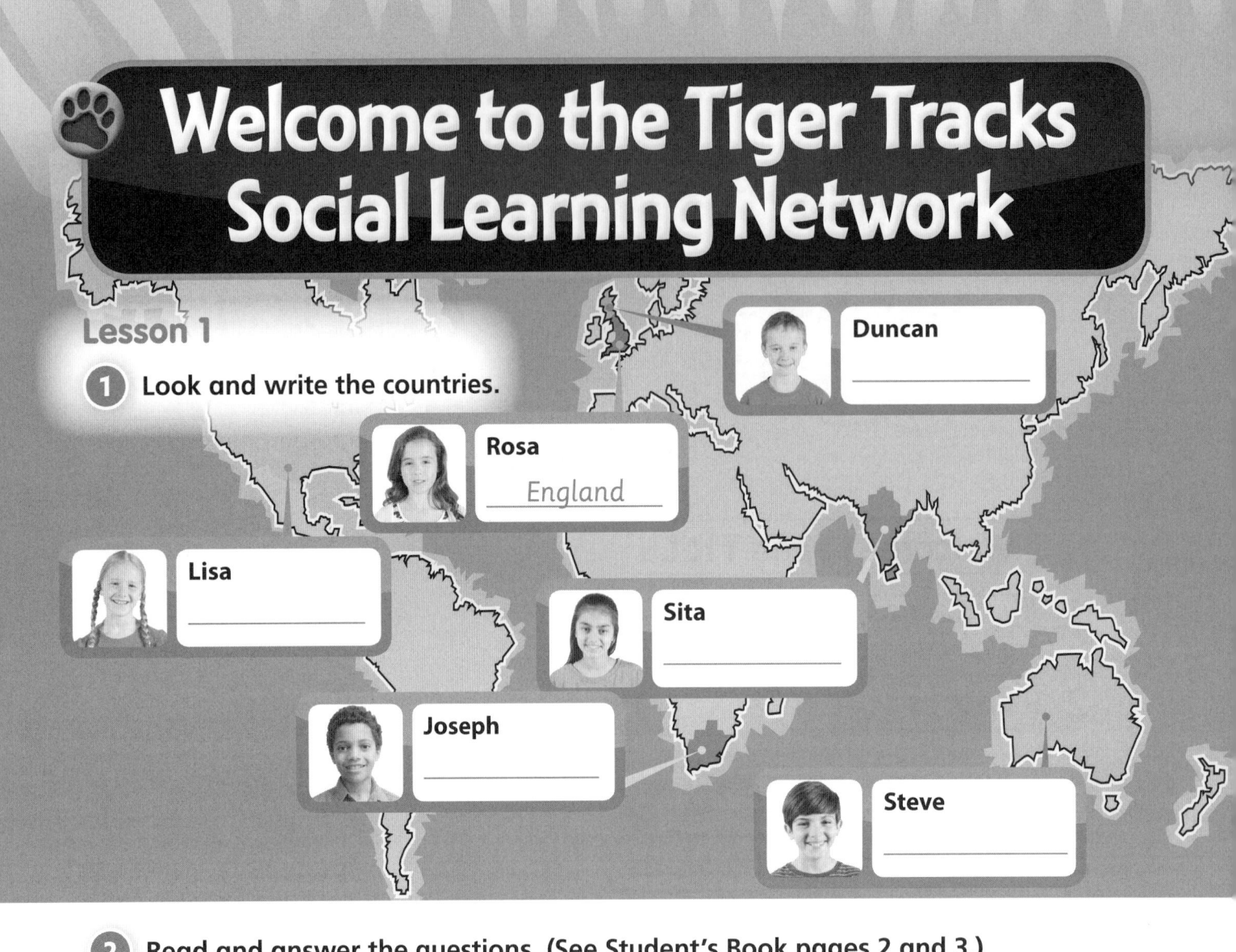

Duncan _____

Rosa _*England*_

Lisa _____

Sita _____

Joseph _____

Steve _____

2 Read and answer the questions. (See Student's Book pages 2 and 3.)

1 When's Rosa's birthday? _It's on March 18th._

2 How old is Steve? _____

3 What does Sita love? _____

4 What's Lisa's favorite food? _____

5 What's Duncan's favorite subject? _____

6 When's Joseph's birthday? _____

3 Match and say.

1st   20th   twentieth   2nd   thirtieth   twenty-first

twenty-third   eighth   3rd   21st   24th   22nd   ninth   5th

4th   twelfth   23rd   twenty-second   fifth   third   second

9th   first   fourth   8th   30th   twenty-fourth   12th

Lesson 2

4 01:05 **Listen and write.**

Name: _____James_____

Age: _____

Country: _____

Birthday: _____

Likes: _____

Favorite subject: _____

Favorite food: _____

5 **Order and write the questions.** **Ask a friend and write the answers.**

1 your / name / What's / ? *What's your name?*_____
_____

2 old / How / you / are / ? _____
_____

3 you / from / are / Where / ? _____
_____

4 do / What / like / you / ? _____
_____

5 your / birthday / When's / ? _____
_____

6 subject / your / What's / favorite / ? _____
_____

7 favorite / What's / food / your / ? _____
_____

6 **Read and write about your friend.**

Lisa is eleven years old. She's from the U.S. Lisa likes music and movies. Her birthday is on September 30th. Her favorite subject is English and her favorite food is pizza.

_____
_____
_____
_____
_____

1 🐾 A world of gadgets

Lesson 1

1 Look and write. Find the missing gadget.

¹ F L A S H ▮ D R I V E

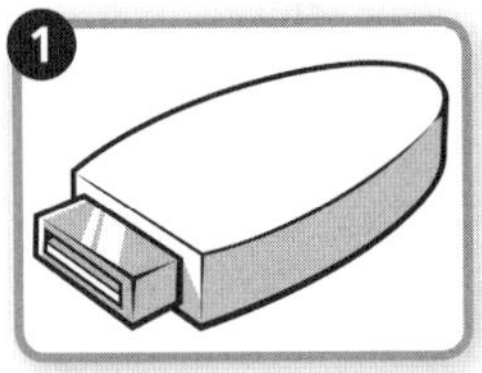

2

3

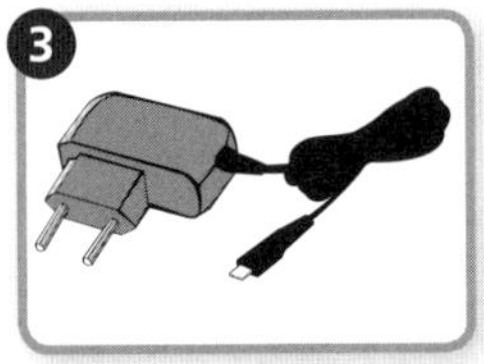

4

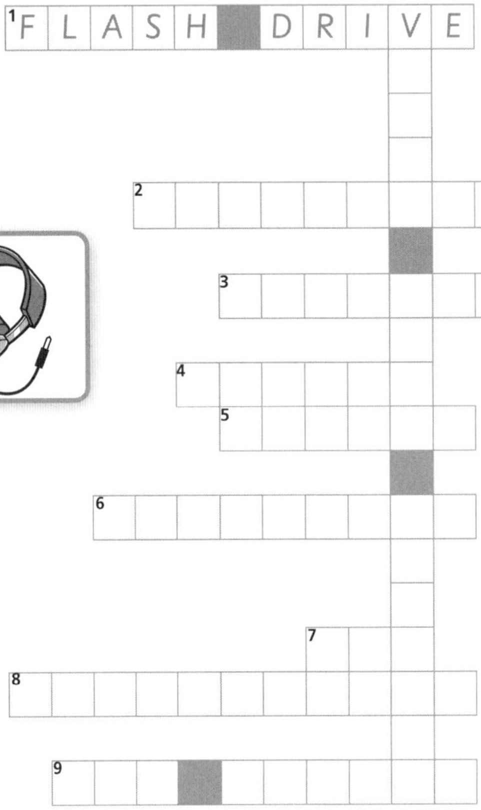

5

6

7

8

9

2 ♻ Write questions. Answer *Yes, I do* or *No, I don't*.

1 <u>Do you have a TV?</u> _____

2 _____ _____

3 _____ _____

4 _____ _____

5 _____ _____

3 Write about the gadgets.

1 <u>You use this to do math.</u> _____

2 _____

3 _____

4 _____

Lesson 2

4 Read and circle. (See Student's Book page 5.)

1 The Fab Tab is **big** / **small.**
2 The Fab Tab is **light** / **heavy**.
3 The Fab Tab is **difficult** / **easy** to use.
4 The Fab Tab is **fun** / **boring**.

5 Read and write. (See Student's Book page 5.)

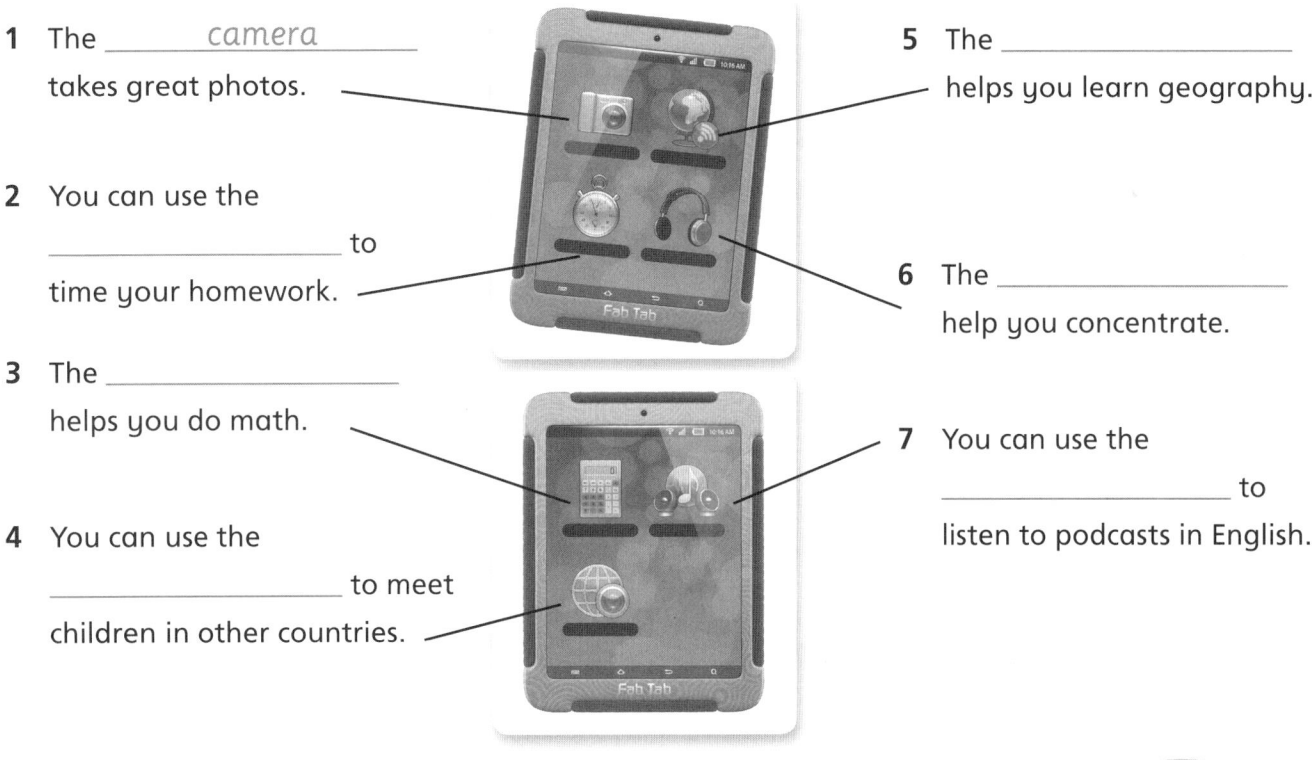

1 The _____camera_____ takes great photos.

2 You can use the _____ to time your homework.

3 The _____ helps you do math.

4 You can use the _____ to meet children in other countries.

5 The _____ helps you learn geography.

6 The _____ help you concentrate.

7 You can use the _____ to listen to podcasts in English.

6 Listen and complete. Write.
01:10

1 I think the Fab Tab is _great_ . I want to use a Fab Tab to _do projects_ .

2 I think the Fab Tab is _____ . I want to use a Fab Tab to _____ .

3 I think the Fab Tab is _____ . I want to use a Fab Tab to _____ .

4 I think the Fab Tab is _____ . I want to use a Fab Tab to _____ .

And you? I think _____ . I want to _____ .

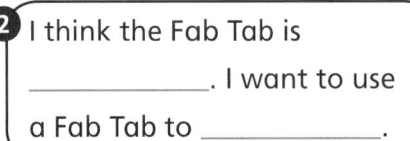

Lesson 3

7 **Read the story and write the answers.**
(See Student's Book page 6.) Ask and say.

Picture 1: What does Alan do in three weeks? _Alan learns to read._

Picture 2: What does Alan love doing? _____

Picture 3: What does Alan use math to calculate? _____

Picture 4: How old is Alan when he starts middle school?_____

Picture 5: What does Alan study at Cambridge University? _____

Picture 6: Where does Alan work after college? _____

Picture 7: What's the name of the code Alan helps to crack? _____

Picture 8: What does Alan develop at Manchester University? _____

Picture 9: What is Alan's work important for today? _____

8 **Look and write the message.**

Do you enjoy secret codes like Alan Turing? Can you work out the message?

| YA DOTE SUEW TAHT STEG DAGC INOR |
| TCEL EROF TNAT ROPM ISIS EDOC TERC |
| ESDN AECN EICS RETU PMOC NOKR |
| OWS'G NIRU TNAL A |

Alan _____

_____

_____

_____

9 **Read and circle. Write a review of the story. Tell your family about the story.**

1 The story is **a science fiction story /** (**a biography**).

2 The story is about a famous **Englishman / Australian**.

3 At school, Alan Turing is very good at **English and art / math and science**.

4 At college, Alan studies **history / math**.

5 After college, Alan works on **secret codes and computers / art and history**.

6 Today he is called the father of **computer science / puzzles**.

The story is a _biography_ of a famous _____. At school, _____ _____. At college, _____.

After college, _____ _____. Today he is called _____.

I think Alan Turing is _____ _____.

My favorite part of the story is when _____.

I _____ this story. It's _____.

 = **Home-School Link**

Lesson 4

10 Write sentences. (See Student's Book page 8.)

1 Lucy _____ *Lucy sometimes uses her tablet.* _____

2 Zak _____

3 Lucy _____

4 Zak _____

5 Lucy _____

11 Read and write. Be a grammar detective!

Adverbs of frequency
- We use adverbs of frequency to talk about how often we do things.
- We put adverbs of frequency:
  - before the main verb e.g. *I sometimes use a GPS.*
  - before the auxiliary verb in answers e.g. *Does she …? Yes, she always does.*

1 _____

2 _____

3 _____ often _____

4 _____

0%   100%

12 Write true sentences about you. Use adverbs of frequency.

1 _____ *I sometimes use a flash drive.* _____

2 _____

3 _____

4 _____

5 _____

6 _____

Lesson 5

13 Remember and write. 🔊 Listen, underline /tʃ/ and /dʒ/ and count.
01:16

Jamie _____

_____

_____

_____

_____ ☐

Charlie _____

_____

_____

_____

_____ ☐

Which consonants do we use to pronounce /tʃ/ in the sentences? _____

Which consonants do we use to pronounce /dʒ/ in the sentences? _____

14 Write questions and answers. (See Student's Book page 9.)

1 Ben   Does Ben watch TV on Saturday?   Yes, he often does.

2 Lyn   _____   _____

3 Sam   _____   _____

4 Jo   _____   _____

5 Ben   _____   _____

6 Jo   _____   _____

15 🏠 Write about your friends or family. Tell your family.

1 (watch TV)   My father always watches TV after dinner.

2 (go shopping)   _____

3 (do homework)   _____

4 (use a computer)   _____

5 (play soccer)   _____

6 (read books)   _____

 = Home-School Link

Lesson 6

16 **Read and write O (Oxford) or C (Cambridge). (See Student's Book page 10.)**

1 The dining room of a college is Hogwarts Hall. __O__

2 It has a glasshouse with carnivorous plants. _____

3 It has a large deer park. _____

4 You can see ancient Egyptian mummies. _____

5 You can see traditional costumes. _____

6 You can walk in a beautiful park by the river. _____

17 🔊 **Listen and write.**
01:19

Rosa uses the Tiger Tracks SLN to talk to a college student.   POST ☑

Name: _____ Ryan _____   Age: _____

Name of university: _____

Studying: _____

Loves: _____

Wants to work in: _____ or _____

Lesson 7
Everyday chit-chat

18 **Read and complete the dialogue in your own words.** 🔲 **Act out.**

Woman: Hello there. (1) *Can I help you?* _____

You: Oh, yes, please. I need a (2) _____.

Woman: OK. Come this way, please. All the

(3) _____ are over here.

You: Oh, great. I think this is the one I need.

How (4) _____?

Woman: This one is (5) _____.

You: OK. Here you go. (6) _____ exactly.

Woman: Perfect. (7) _____

Lesson 8

19 **Read and write the missing words. (See Student's Book page 12.)**

creative ~~lifestyle~~ concentrate cons skills

1 If you always use electronic gadgets and never do anything else, you need to change your ___lifestyle___.

2 There are many pros and _____ about electronic gadgets.

3 Electronic gadgets improve your keyboard _____.

4 Electronic gadgets make you more _____.

5 You sometimes find it hard to _____ on school work.

20 **Order and write. Write *P* (pro) or *C* (con).**

1 improve / They / skills / keyboard / your
   _They improve your keyboard skills.___ | P |

2 time / You / outdoor / have / activities / for / don't
   _____ | ☐ |

3 creative / make / They / more / you
   _____ | ☐ |

4 subjects / They / learn / you / school / help
   _____ | ☐ |

21 🔊 01:24 **Listen and check (✓).**

Lisa is asking the Tiger Tracks SLN members their opinions about the article on electronic gadgets.

Agrees with ...	Steve	Sita	Rosa	Duncan	Joseph
the pros	✓				
the cons					
the pros and the cons					

22 🏠 **Write your opinion about the article. Tell your family.**   *My opinion*

I agree with _____.

I think _____.

🏠 **= Home-School Link**

Project: Electronic gadget survey

23 Read Lisa's project and complete the table. (See Student's Book page 13.)

Lisa

Lisa's mom

Get ready for your project

	always	usually	often	sometimes	never
cell phone	mom				
tablet		dad			
video game console			aunt	grandad	
GPS					
MP3 player					dad

24 Choose the people and gadgets for your survey.

_____ _____ _____ _____

Prepare your project

My electronic gadget survey					
Gadgets	always	usually	often	sometimes	never
_____					
_____					
_____					
_____					

Now carry out your survey!

25 Read your notes and write your survey report.

Write your project in your notebook

Think!
- Start with the aim of your survey.

Writing Tip!
- Use a new paragraph to write about each person.

Remember!
- Put adverbs of frequency before the main verb.

The aim of my survey is …

Unit review and self-assessment

26 🔊 01:26 **Listen and number. Write the names of the electronic gadgets.**

calculator □	music player □	game console □	GPS 1	smartphone □
webcam □	USB □	headphones □	charger □	stopwatch □

1 It's a <u>GPS</u>.

2 It's a _____.

3 It's a _____.

4 It's an _____.

5 It's a _____.

6 It's a _____.

7 It's a _____.

8 It's a _____.

9 It's a _____.

10 They're _____.

27 **Look and write sentences.**

Things Lisa does on Saturday

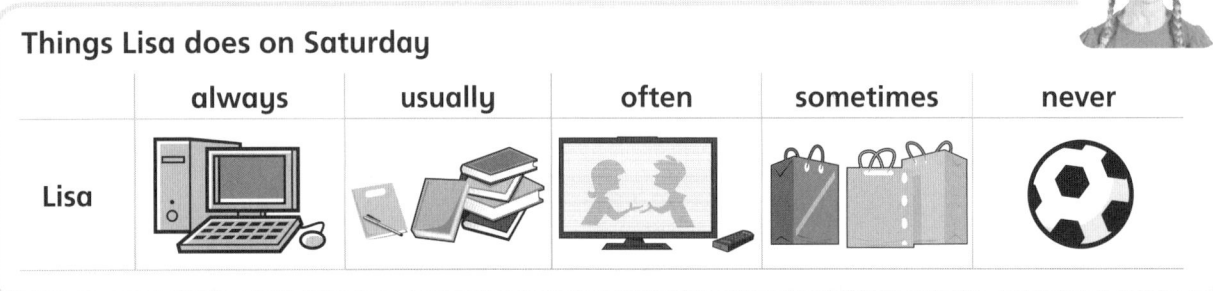

	always	usually	often	sometimes	never
Lisa	computer	books	TV	shopping	football

1 Lisa <u>always uses a computer</u> on Saturday.

2 _____

3 _____

4 _____

5 _____

28 **Write questions and answers. (See Student's Book page 8.)**

1 Lucy 🎧 *Does Lucy use headphones?*   *Yes, she always does.*

2 Zak 💻 _____   _____

3 Lucy 🎵 _____   _____

4 Zak 📷 _____   _____

5 Lucy ⏱ _____   _____

6 Zak 📱 _____   _____

29 **Read and write the answers. (See Student's Book page 10.)**

1 What's the capital of England? _____

2 Who is on every English stamp? _____

3 What color are English mailboxes? _____

4 What's the name of the river in London? _____

5 What's England's favorite food? _____

6 What's the most popular country for a vacation? _____

30 **Write sentences about the pros of electronic gadgets. Use these words. (See Student's Book page 12.)**

~~keyboard skills~~ creative school subjects the world

1 *Electronic gadgets improve your keyboard skills.*

2 *Electronic gadgets* _____

3 _____

4 _____

Assess your work in Unit 1.

Look and circle. 🙂 🙂 😐 🙁 ☹

Complete your *Progress Journal* for Unit 1.

13

2 🐾 Sports scene

Lesson 1

1 Find, circle and write.

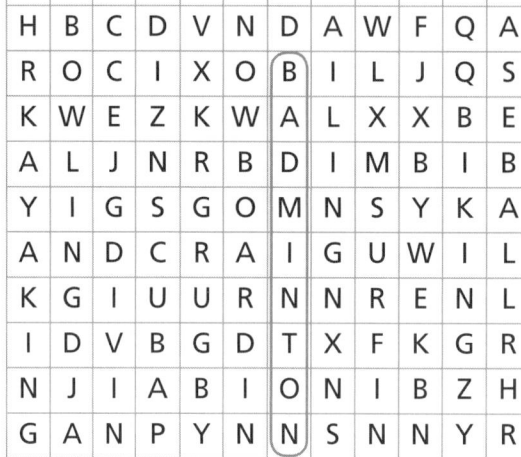

Y	F	F	Q	H	S	G	S	P	S	K	B
H	B	C	D	V	N	D	A	W	F	Q	A
R	O	C	I	X	O	B	I	L	J	Q	S
K	W	E	Z	K	W	A	L	X	X	B	E
A	L	J	N	R	B	D	I	M	B	I	B
Y	I	G	S	G	O	M	N	S	Y	K	A
A	N	D	C	R	A	I	G	U	W	I	L
K	G	I	U	U	R	N	N	R	E	N	L
I	D	V	B	G	D	T	X	F	K	G	R
N	J	I	A	B	I	O	N	I	B	Z	H
G	A	N	P	Y	N	N	S	N	N	Y	R
W	K	G	Z	Y	G	F	J	G	E	R	E

1 badminton
2 _____
3 _____
4 _____
5 _____
6 _____
7 _____
8 _____
9 _____
10 _____

2 ♻ Write questions. Answer *Yes, I do* or *No, I don't*.

1 ⚽ <u>Do you like soccer?</u> _____ _____

2 🎾 _____ _____

3 🥽 _____ _____

4 🛹 _____ _____

5 🏀 _____ _____

3 Write about the sports.

1 <u>In baseball, you hit a ball with a bat.</u>

2 _____

3 _____

4 _____

Lesson 2

4 **Read and write *T* (true) or *F* (false). (See Student's Book page 15.)**

1 You see baseball on the sports tour. _F_

2 You see crocodiles on the city tour. _____

3 You see waterfalls on the outback tour. _____

4 You see kangaroos on the rainforest tour. _____

5 You see rugby on the sports tour. _____

6 You see koalas on the rainforest tour. _____

5 **Read and write. Invent your own city tour.**

My city tour

On this tour, we visit the fantastic city of Madrid.

We visit the famous Prado Museum and walk in the beautiful Retiro Park.

We also visit Madrid Zoo. It's famous for its panda bears.

My city tour

On this tour, we visit (1) _____

_____.

We visit (2) _____

and walk (3) _____.

We also visit (4) _____.

It's famous for (5) _____

_____.

6 **Listen and complete. Write.**
01:31

1 I want to go on the _____sports_____ tour to _____go surfing_____.

2 I want to go on the _____ tour to _____.

3 I want to go on the _____ tour to _____.

4 I want to go on the _____ tour to _____.

And you? I _____.

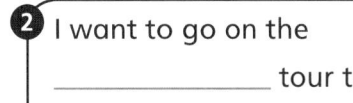
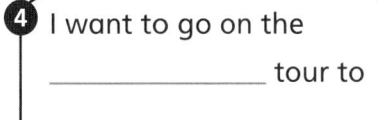

Lesson 3

7 Read the story and write the answers.
(See Student's Book page 16.) 🔁🧍 Ask and say.

Picture 1: What do they have on their bikes? _They have everything._

Picture 2: What does Natalie do when they stop? _____

Picture 3: What are they eating? _____

Picture 4: Where are they staying? _____

Picture 5: What's Jack doing? _____

Picture 6: What stings Mom's ankle? _____

Picture 7: Who's saying 'well done' to Jack? _____

Picture 8: Where are they? _____

Picture 9: What's Jack still doing? _____

8 Read and write. (See Student's Book page 16.)

How to treat scorpion stings

sting   cold   ~~poison~~
heart   bandage   soap

- Wash the (1) _____poison_____ away with (2) _____.
- Put the sting in (3) _____ water.
- Make the person lie down with their (4) _____ above the (5) _____.
- Use a (6) _____ to stop the poison from spreading.

9 🎩 Read and circle. Write a review of the story. Tell your family about the story.

1 The story is (a travel story) / a detective story.

2 The story is about a **car journey across the US** / **bike ride across Australia**.

3 Natalie and her family go from **Sydney to Adelaide** / **Adelaide to Sydney**.

4 The distance is **1,400 kilometers** / **1,600 kilometers**.

5 The journey takes **20 days** / **30 days**.

6 They raise **10,000 dollars** / **3,000 dollars** for charity.

The story is a _____travel story_____ about a _____.

Natalie and her family _____ _____.

The distance _____ and the journey _____.

They raise _____ for charity.

I think Natalie and her family are _____ .

My favorite part of the story is when _____.

I _____ this story. It's _____.

Lesson 4

10 **Write sentences. (See Student's Book page 18.)**

		The good biker	The bad biker
1	(wear)	*She's wearing a helmet.*	*He isn't wearing a helmet.*
2	(wear)		
3	(bike)		
4	(listen)		

11 **Read and write. Be a grammar detective!**

Present continuous tense
- We use the present continuous to talk about things that are happening now.
- We make the present continuous with the verb + *ing* e.g. *play* → *playing*.
- We take away the final *e* e.g. *bike* → *biking*, *write* → *writing*.
- We double the consonant after one vowel, one consonant e.g. *run* → *running*, *hop* → *hopping*.

1	read	*reading*	**7**	hit	
2	fly		**8**	take	
3	swim		**9**	make	
4	sit		**10**	put	
5	watch		**11**	walk	
6	use		**12**	come	

12 **Write true sentences about now.**

1	(write)	*I'm writing.*
2	(bike)	*I'm not biking.*
3	(wear)	
4	(run)	
5	(play)	
6	(listen)	

Lesson 5

13 Remember and write. 🔊 Listen, underline /aɪ/ and /eɪ/
and count.
01:37

 Eileen _____

_____

_____

_____

_____ ☐

 Adrian _____

_____

_____

_____

_____ ☐

Which vowels do we use to pronounce /aɪ/ in the sentences? _____

Which vowels do we use to pronounce /eɪ/ in the sentences? _____

14 Write questions and answers.

1 (play badminton) _Is he playing badminton?_ ___ 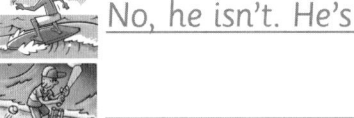 _No, he isn't. He's surfing._

2 (snowboard) _____ _____

3 (play baseball) _____ _____

4 (play rugby) _____ _____

5 (play badminton) _____ _____

6 (surf) _____ _____

15 🏠 Find the differences. Write sentences. Tell your family about the pictures.

A    **B**

1 _A boy is kayaking._ _____

2 _Two girls_ _____

3 _____ _____

Culture

Lesson 6

16 **Read and match. (See Student's Book page 20.)**

1 You use a surfboard with a large sail.
2 You play this on a team and score goals.
3 A motor boat pulls you through the water.
4 You discover the world under the ocean.
5 You ride the waves on a surfboard with a kite.
6 You paddle in a raft on a river with six or eight other people.

a water polo
b kitesurfing
c white water rafting
d windsurfing
e waterskiing
f snorkeling

17 **Listen and match. Write.** 01:40

The Tiger Tracks SLN members tell Steve about water sports they want to try. POST ☑

Lisa   Sita   Rosa   Duncan   Joseph

I want to try _____.

Lesson 7
Everyday chit-chat

18 **Read and complete the dialogue in your own words. Act out.**

You: Good (1) _____afternoon_____. I'd like to find out about (2) _____ coaching.

Man: Can (3) _____? Or are you a beginner?

You: (4) I _____.

Man: Well, we have (5) _____ once a week. It's after school every (6) _____ at _____.

You: That's perfect.

Lesson 8

19 **Read and write the missing words. (See Student's Book page 22.)**

heart   ~~breathe~~   lungs   muscles   blood   joints   muscles

1   When you exercise, you _____breathe_____ fast.

2   Your _____ pumps _____ around your body.

3   The blood carries oxygen from your _____ to your _____.

4   Your _____ help your _____ to move.

20 **Complete the table. Write sentences. (See Student's Book page 22.)**

	Good for ...	Examples
Aerobic exercise	heart	swimming,
Strength training		
Flexibility training		

1   _Aerobic exercise is good for your heart. Examples are swimming,_ _____

_____

2   _____

3   _____

21 🔊 **Listen and complete the table.**
02:01

Steve is asking the Tiger Tracks SLN members about their favorite kind of exercise and the sports they do or play to get it.

	Rosa	Sita	Lisa	Duncan	Joseph
Favorite kind of exercise	aerobic exercise				
Sport	soccer				

22 🏠 **Write about you. Tell your family.**   *My opinion*

My favorite kind of exercise is _____.

I _____ to get _____.

Project: Do I get enough exercise?

Read Duncan's project and complete his exercise diary. (See Student's Book page 23.)

Get ready for your project

	Activities	Approximate time
Monday	walk to school and back home _____	_____ 1 hour
	play at break time	30 minutes
Tuesday	_____	30 minutes
	play at break time	30 minutes
Wednesday	walk to school and back home _____	30 minutes
		30 minutes

Complete your exercise diary.

Prepare your project

	Activities	Approximate time
Monday		
Tuesday		
Wednesday		

Read your exercise diary and write a report.

Think!
- Use a new sentence to write about each day or place where you exercise.

Remember!
- Use the present tense to write about what you do every day.
- Use the present continuous tense to say what you're doing in the photos.

Writing Tip!
- Use *on* for days of the week and the weekend; use *at* for break time.

Write your project in your notebook

Every week, I get ...

Unit review and self-assessment

26 🔊 **Listen and number. Write the names of the sports.**
02:03

1 It's <u>scuba diving</u>.

2 It's _____.

3 It's _____.

4 It's _____.

5 It's _____.

6 It's _____.

7 It's _____.

8 It's _____.

9 It's _____.

10 It's _____.

27 **Look and write sentences.**

1 They're <u>kayaking</u>.

2 _____

3 _____

4 _____

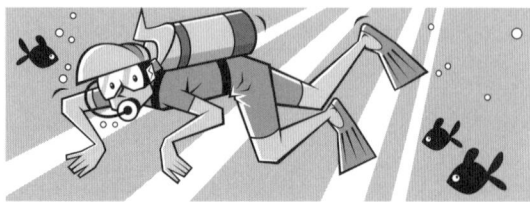 

5 _____

6 _____

28 **Look and write questions and answers**

Sam   Emily   Becky   Chris   Henry

1 (Sam / bowling)   *Is Sam bowling?*   *No, he isn't. He's biking.*

2 (Emily / soccer)   _____   _____

3 (Becky / sailing)   _____   _____

4 (Chris / badminton)   _____   _____

5 (Henry / baseball)   _____   _____

29 **Read and write the answers. (See Student's Book page 20.)**

1 What's the capital of Australia?   _____

2 How many square kilometers is Australia?   _____

3 Which two animals are the symbols of Australia?   _____

4 What's the popular name for the Sydney Harbour Bridge? _____

5 How high is Uluru?   _____

6 How many sheep are there in Australia?   _____

30 **Answer the questions. (See Student's Book page 22.)**

1 What is one positive effect of regular exercise?
   You build strong muscles.

2 What is aerobic exercise good for?
   _____

3 What is strength training good for?
   _____

4 What is flexibility training good for?
   _____

Assess your work in Unit 2.

Look and circle.   ☺

Complete your *Progress Journal* for Unit 2.

3 🐾 Awesome animals

Lesson 1

1 **Read and write.**

1 It's very tall. It has long legs and a long beak.
What is it? <u>It's a flamingo</u>

2 It has big ears and red fur. It has a long tail with brown stripes.
What is it? _____

3 It has soft, black fur. It's fierce. It runs very fast.
What is it? _____

4 It's very big and very fierce. It lives near rivers.
What is it? _____

5 It's very big and it has a long horn.
What is it? _____

6 It has white fur with black spots and sharp teeth.
What is it? _____

2 ♻ **Write questions and answers.**

1 <u>Do tigers live in India?</u> <u>Yes, they do.</u>

2 _____ _____

3 _____ _____

4 _____ _____

3 **Write about the animals.**

1 <u>An eagle has big wings and a big beak.</u>
<u>It also has sharp claws.</u>

2 _____
_____

3 _____
_____

4 _____
_____

❶ ❷

❸ ❹

Lesson 2

4 **Read and write. (See Student's Book page 25.)**

Animals in national parks near rivers and forests:

elephants,

Animals in national parks in the mountains:

bears,

5 **Order and write the questions. Write short answers. (See Student's Book page 25.)**

National parks near rivers and forests

1 hot / the / Is / summer / in / it / ?   _Is it hot in the summer?_   _Yes, it is._

2 season / Is / a / monsoon / there / ? _____ _____

3 tigers / you / Can / see / ?   _____ _____

National parks in the mountains

4 lot / a / Is / snow / of / there / ?   _____ _____

5 long / Is / summer / the / ?   _____ _____

6 snow leopards / have / Do / spots / ? _____ _____

6 🔊 **Listen and complete. Write.**

02:08

TALK ABOUT IT!

1 I want to go to a park _near rivers and forests_ because I want to see ___ _a tiger_ ___.

2 I want to go to a park _____ _____ because I want to see _____.

3 I want to go to a park _____ _____ because I want to see _____.

4 I want to go to a park _____ _____ because I want to see _____.

And you?   I _____.

Lesson 3

7 Read the story and write the answers.
(See Student's Book page 26.) 👥 **Ask and say.**

Picture 1: Do tigers have stripes? <u>No, they don't.</u>

Picture 2: What is the man doing? _____

Picture 3: What does the tiger want? _____

Picture 4: How is the man feeling? _____

Picture 5: Where does the man tie the tiger? _____

Picture 6: What do the man and his son bring? _____

Picture 7: Who sets the straw on fire? _____

Picture 8: What color are the tiger's stripes? _____

Picture 9: Do tigers trust people? _____

8 Write sentences about the story. Use these words.

> ~~buffalo~~ curious hungry
> straw rope river

1 <u>The buffalo is eating grass.</u>

2 _____

3 _____

4 _____

5 _____

6 _____

9 🏠 **Read and circle. Write a review of the story. Tell your family about the story.**

1 The story is (traditional) /
a fairy tale.

2 The story is from **India / Africa**.

3 The story is about how the tiger
got its **claws / stripes**.

4 At the start of the story,
the tiger doesn't have any
stripes / paws.

5 At the end of the story,
the tiger has **brown and
yellow stripes / orange
and black stripes**.

The story is a ___<u>traditional</u>___ story from
_____. It's about how _____
_____. At the start of the story,
_____. At the end of the story,
_____.

My favorite character in the story is _____
_____. My favorite part of the story is when
_____.
I _____ this story. It's _____
_____.

Lesson 4

10 **Read and write correct sentences. (See Student's Book page 28.)**

1 The Asian elephant is bigger.

   <u>No, it isn't. The African elephant</u>
   <u>is bigger.</u>

2 The Asian elephant is taller.

   <u>No, _____</u>

3 The Asian elephant has longer legs.

   <u>No, it doesn't. _____</u>

4 The African elephant has smaller ears.

   _____

African elephant

Asian elephant

11 **Read and write. Be a grammar detective!**

Comparative adjectives

- We use comparative adjectives when we compare animals, people and things.
- When an adjective has:
  – one syllable, we add *-er* e.g. *tall* ➔ *taller*.
  – one vowel and one consonant at the end, we double the consonant e.g. *big* ➔ *bigger*.
  – two syllables ending in *y*, we change the *y* to *i* e.g. *heavy* ➔ *heavier*.
  – three or more syllables, we use *more* e.g. *intelligent* ➔ *more intelligent*.

1	_strong_	stronger
2	_____	bigger
heavy	3	_____
4	_____	more intelligent

long	5	_____
hot	6	_____
7	_____	funnier
beautiful	8	_____

12 **Write sentences to compare the animals.**

1 (tall) <u>An elephant is taller than a hippo.</u>

2 (big wings) _____

3 (heavy) _____

4 (long neck) _____

Lesson 5

13 Remember and write. 🔊 02:14 Listen, underline /ə/ and count.

My sister's _____

_____

_____

_____

_____ ☐

My mother's _____

_____

_____

_____

_____ ☐

Which letters do we sometimes pronounce as /ə/?

_____

14 Write sentences. (See Student's Book page 29).

1 (Lia / Jen / short)   Lia is shorter than Jen.

2 (Spike / Tom / light hair) Spike has lighter hair than Tom.

3 (Tom / Spike / tall)   _____

4 (Jen / Lia / curly hair)   _____

5 (Spike / Tom / young)   _____

6 (Jen / Spike / long hair) _____

15 🏠 Write about you and your friends or family. Tell your family about your friends at school.

1 (old)   I'm older than _____

2 (tall)   _____

3 (long hair) _____

4 (young)   _____

5 (short)   _____

6 (curly hair) _____

Culture

Lesson 6

16 **Read and answer the questions. (See Student's Book page 30.)**

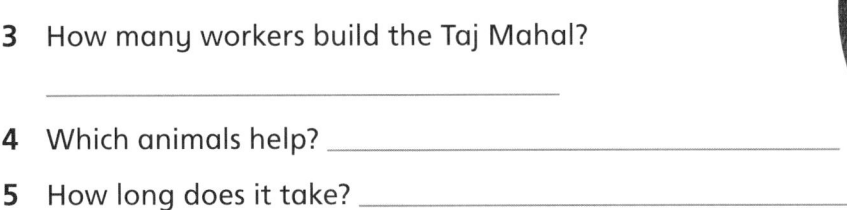

1 Who builds the Taj Mahal? _The Emperor of India._

2 Who is the Taj Mahal in memory of?

_____

3 How many workers build the Taj Mahal?

_____

4 Which animals help? _____

5 How long does it take? _____

6 What is the Taj Mahal made of? _____

7 What is it decorated with? _____

8 What color is the Taj Mahal in the early morning? _____

17 🔊 02:17 **Listen, number and write.**

The Tiger Tracks SLN members tell Sita about famous buildings in their country. POST ✓

Big Ben
_____

Sydney Opera House
_____

Empire State Building
the US

Edinburgh Castle
_____

My favorite famous building in my country is _____.

Lesson 7
Everyday chit-chat

18 **Read and complete the dialogue in your own words.** 🔁 **Act out.**

Man: How can I help you?

You: I'd like (1) _____two tickets_____ to visit the (2) _____, please.

Man: Is that for adults or children? Tickets for children under sixteen are cheaper.

You: Oh, thanks. It's for (3) _____ and (4) _____, please.

Man: OK. That's (5) _____ dollars in total, please.

You: Here (6) _____.

Man: Thank you.

29

Lesson 8

19 **Read, write and match. (See Student's Book page 32.)**

forests   trash   tusks   ~~hotter~~

1   The Earth is getting ___hotter___ . $\boxed{C}$

2   The Earth, rivers and oceans are full of chemicals and _____ . $\boxed{}$

3   Animals lose their homes when people cut down _____ . $\boxed{}$

4   People kill wild animals for their skins, horns or _____ . $\boxed{}$

A   Loss of habitat   **B**   Hunting and poaching   **C**   Global warming   **D**   Pollution

20 **Read and write. (See Student's Book page 32.) Ask and say.**

Animal	Where do they live?	How many are there?	Why are they endangered?
mountain gorillas	Africa		
polar bears			
tigers		4,000	
giant pandas			
Indian rhinos			hunting and poaching
snow leopards			

21 🔊 **Listen and circle.**
02:22

Lisa is asking Sita about Asian elephants.

1   Asian elephants are ⟨endangered⟩ / not endangered.

2   Asian elephants live in **mountains** / **forests**.

3   Today there are about **50,000** / **70,000**.

4   They are endangered because of **pollution** / **loss of habitat**.

5   They're also endangered because of **hunting and poaching** / **road traffic**.

22 🔼 **Write about Asian elephants. Tell your family.**   *My opinion*

Asian elephants _____

_____

_____ .

Project: An endangered animal

23 **Read Lisa's project and make notes. (See Student's Book page 33.)**

Get ready for your project

Lisa's favorite endangered animal:	the red wolf
Where they live:	
Appearance:	
Food:	
Character:	
Why they're in danger:	
How they compare with gray wolves:	
How many there are in the US:	

24 **Choose, research and make notes.**

Prepare your project

My favorite endangered animal:	
Where they live:	
Appearance:	
Food:	
Character:	
Why they're in danger:	
How they compare with another animal:	
How many there are today:	

25 **Read your notes and write.**

Think!
- How many paragraphs do you need?

Writing Tip!
- Keep sentences short. Use *also* to add ideas.

Write your project in your notebook

Remember!
- To compare, write ... *er than* ...
- To give reasons, write *because of* ...

My favorite endangered animal is ...

Unit review and self-assessment

26 🔊 02:24 **Listen and number. Write the names of the animals.**

1 It's an _eagle_____.

2 It's a _____.

3 It's a _____.

4 It's a _____.

5 It's a _____.

6 It's a _____.

7 It's a _____.

8 It's a _____.

9 It's a _____.

10 It's a _____.

27 **Write sentences.**

Asian lion
– small and light
– short body
– short, dark mane

African lion
– strong and heavy
– long body
– long, thick mane

1 The Asian lion is _smaller_____ than _the African lion_____.

2 The Asian lion has a _____.

3 _____

4 The African lion is _____.

5 _____

6 _____

28 Write questions and answers.

Lisa
I'm eleven years old.
I'm 1.50 meters tall.
I have light hair.

Sita
I'm twelve years old.
I'm 1.53 meters tall.
I have dark hair.

1 (Sita / old)   Is Sita older than Lisa?   Yes, she is.

2 (Sita / light hair)   Does Sita have lighter hair than Lisa?   No, she doesn't.

3 (Lisa / tall)   _____   _____

4 (Lisa / short)   _____   _____

5 (Lisa / young)   _____   _____

6 (Sita / dark hair)   _____   _____

29 Read and write the answers. (See Student's Book page 30.)

1 What's the capital of India?   _____

2 What's the national animal of India?   _____

3 Which language do many people speak?   _____

4 How many official languages are there?   _____

5 What's India's favorite drink?   _____

6 What's the name of India's movie industry?   _____

30 Look and write sentences. (See Student's Book page 32.)

1 Polar bears and tigers are endangered because of global warming.

2 _____

3 _____

4 _____

Assess your work in Unit 3.

Look and circle.

Complete your *Progress Journal* for Unit 3.

4 🐾 People and professions

Lesson 1

1 **Read and write.**

1 This person is a professional cook.

He's a _____chef_____.

2 This person works in politics and government.

She's a _____.

3 This person has original ideas and makes new things.

He's an _____.

4 This person writes for newspapers and websites.

She's a _____.

5 This person plays an instrument and writes music.

He's a _____.

6 This person acts in movies.

She's a _____.

2 ♻ **Write questions. Answer _Yes, I do_ or _No, I don't_.**

1 _Do you want to be a teacher?_ _____

2 _____ _____

3 _____ _____

4 _____ _____

3 **Write about the professions.**

1 _A scientist works in science._

2 _____

3 _____

4 _____

Lesson 2

4 **Read and write correct sentences. (See Student's Book page 35.)**

 1  2  3  4

1 Selena Gomez is a journalist. _No, she isn't. She's a singer, an actor and a fashion designer._

2 Mark Zuckerberg is a scientist. _____

3 Kobe Bryant is a soccer player. _____

4 Michelle Obama is a doctor. _____

5 **Write sentences. Use these words. (See Student's Book page 35.)**

~~bilingual~~ businessman fans wife

1 _Selena Gomez is bilingual in English and Spanish._
2 _Mark Zuckerberg_ _____
3 _Kobe Bryant_ _____
4 _Michelle Obama_ _____

6 **Listen and complete. Write.**
02:29

		Who they admire	Reason
Rosa		Michelle Obama	She promotes healthy eating.
Sita			
Duncan			
Joseph			
And you?		I _____.	

Lesson 3

7 **Read the story and write the answers. (See Student's Book page 36.)** 👤👤 **Ask and say.**

Picture 1: Who was James Marshall? _James Marshall was a builder._

Picture 2: What was Amy's father? _____

Picture 3: Who was very happy? _____

Picture 4: Where were Amy and her family? _____

Picture 5: Where was Amy's father for several months? _____

Picture 6: What was Amy's idea? _____

Picture 7: What was Amy's mother? _____

Picture 8: Why was Amy's father disappointed? _____

Picture 9: What was there more gold from? _____

8 **Order and write the sentences.**

1 was / Amy's / excited / father / very   _Amy's father was very excited._

2 journey / in / was / long / a / The / wagon   _____

3 mother / worried / her / Amy / were / and   _____

4 wild / Many / and / miners / violent / were   _____

5 rivers / The / full / gold / weren't / of   _____

9 🎁 **Read and circle. Write a review of the story. Tell your family about the story.**

1 The story is (a historical story) / a travel story.

2 The story is about the **Silver Rush in Nevada / Gold Rush in California**.

3 Amy and her family travel to California **by train / in a wagon**.

4 Amy's father finds **a lot of gold / only a little gold**.

5 While he's away, Amy's mother is **a baker / a teacher**.

6 At the end of the story, Amy's **mother / father** has more gold.

The story is a ___historical story___ about the
_____.

Amy and her family _____
_____. Amy's father _____
_____. While he's away, _____
_____. At the end of the
story, Amy's _____.

I think Amy and her family are _____
_____.

My favorite part of the story is when _____
_____.

I _____ this story. It's
_____.

36

Lesson 4

10 **Write sentences. (See Student's Book page 38.)**

Sarah and Tom

Jim and Kate

1   (Sarah / cook)   _Sarah was a cook._
2   (Jim and Kate / poor)   _Jim and Kate were poor._
3   (Tom / carpenter)   _____
4   (Sarah and Tom / Ireland) _____
5   (Kate / maid)   _____
6   (Jim and Kate / Australia) _____

11 **Read and write. Be a grammar detective!**

Past tense of be
- We use *was* for *I / he / she / it* in questions, affirmative sentences and short answers.
- We use *were* for *you / we / they* in questions, affirmative sentences and short answers.
- We use *wasn't* (*was not*) and *weren't* (*were not*) in negative sentences and short answers.

Chong and Ling (1) ___were___ from China. Before the gold rush, they (2) _____ poor and unhappy. Chong (3) _____ a farmer and Ling (4) _____ a baker. Chong and Ling (5) _____ in California in 1849. It (6) _____ very exciting. After the gold rush, they (7) _____ rich and happy. They (8) _____ very lucky.

12 **Complete the questions and answers.**

Before the gold rush:

1   __Was__ Sarah a cook?
    Yes, _she was_____.

2   _____ Jim a carpenter?
    No, _____.

3   _____ Sarah and Tom poor?
    Yes, _____.

4   _____ Jim and Kate unhappy?
    No, _____.

After the gold rush:

5   _____ Tom and Sarah rich and happy?
    Yes, _____.

6   _____ Jim and Kate lucky?
    No, _____.

Lesson 5

13 Count the syllables. Sort and write the words. 🔊 02:35 Listen and check.

rich

actor

inventor

builder

wild

scientist

musician

dangerous

scared

unlucky

journalist

One syllable	Two syllables	Three syllables
rich	_____	_____
_____	_____	_____
_____	_____	_____
_____	_____	_____
_____	_____	_____
	_____	_____

lucky

happy

worried

poor

easy

exciting

old

14 Write questions and answers. (See Student's Book page 39.)

1 (Jessica / naughty) _Was Jessica naughty?_
   No, she wasn't. She was happy and easy to please.

2 (Ryan's favorite food / chicken) _____

_____

3 (Laura's favorite toy / red car) _____

_____

4 (Nicholas / noisy) _____

_____

5 (Tina's favorite food / spaghetti) _____

_____

6 (Adam / shy) _____

_____

15 🏠 Read and write about you. Tell your family.

> When I was little, I was very happy and easy to please. My favorite food was spaghetti. My favorite toy was my red bike.

When I _____

_____

_____ .

Culture

Lesson 6

16 **Read and answer the questions. (See Student's Book page 40.)**

1 What is the official currency of the US? <u>The United States dollar.</u>

2 How many cents are there to a dollar? _____

3 What does each dollar bill have on it? _____

4 Who is on the one-dollar bill? _____

5 What are US dollar bills made of? _____

6 What is the same about all dollar bills? _____

17 🔊 02:38 **Listen, match and write. Write about the money in your country.**

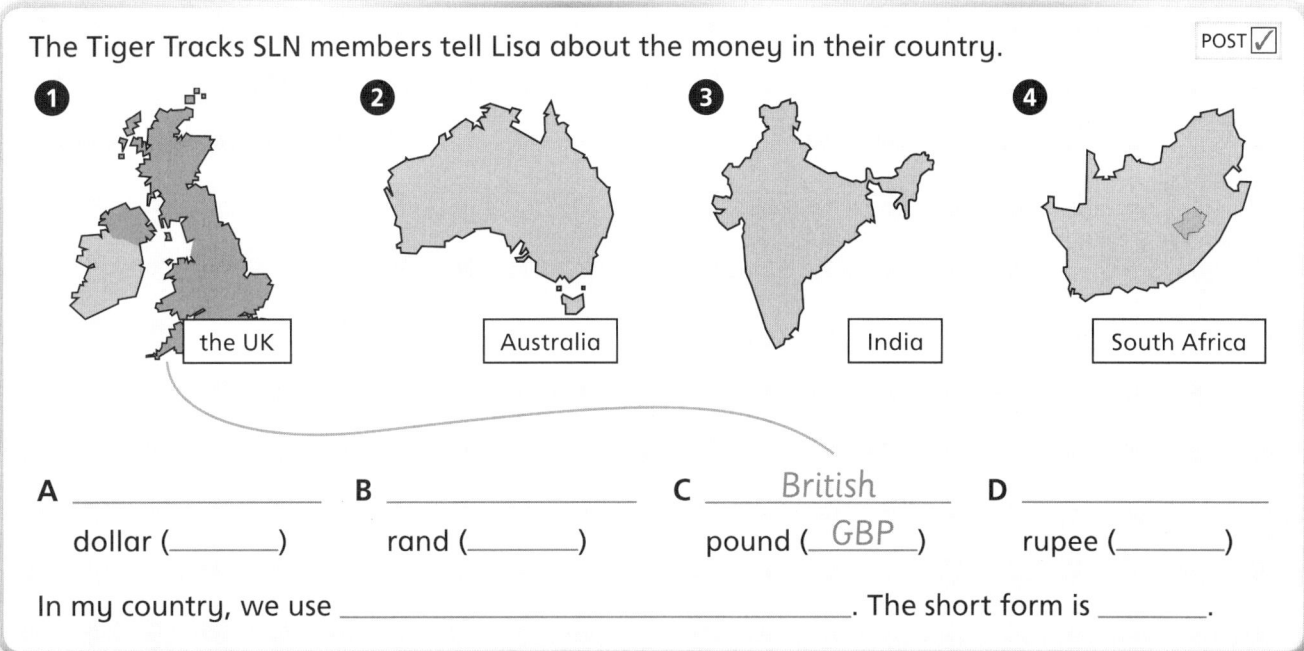

The Tiger Tracks SLN members tell Lisa about the money in their country.   POST ✓

❶ the UK   ❷ Australia   ❸ India   ❹ South Africa

A _____   B _____   C ___<u>British</u>___   D _____
dollar (_____)   rand (_____)   pound (<u>GBP</u>)   rupee (_____)

In my country, we use _____. The short form is _____.

Lesson 7
Everyday chit-chat

18 **Read and complete the dialogue in your own words.** 🚶 **Act out.**

Man: (1) <u>Hello.</u>   Do you want to buy (2) _____?

You: Oh, yes, please. It's for (3) _____.
And I'd like this (4) _____ as well,
please. How much is it altogether?

Man: Well, that's (5) _____ altogether.

You: Here's (6) _____. Let me look in my
bag to see if I have some change.

Man: (7) _____

CLIL **Music**

Lesson 8

19 Look and write the names of the music. (See Student's Book page 42.)

Timeline of American music

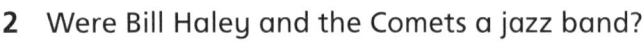

| 1900s | 1920s | 1950s | 1970s |

1 _____jazz_____   2 _____   3 _____   4 _____

20 Read and write the answers. (See Student's Book page 42.)

1 Was Ella Fitzgerald a rock 'n' roll singer?
  No, she wasn't. She was a jazz singer.

2 Were Bill Haley and the Comets a jazz band?
  _____

3 Was Elvis Presley a rap singer?
  _____

4 Was Louis Armstrong a country and western singer?
  _____

5 Were the New Orleans Rhythm Kings a rock 'n' roll band?
  _____

21 🔊 Listen and check (✓).
02:44

Lisa is asking the Tiger Tracks SLN members about music they like.

	rap	dance	pop
Rosa		✓	
Sita			
Steve			
Joseph			

22 🏠 Write about music you like. Tell your family.

My opinion

_____

_____

Project: Quiz on famous people in history

23 **Read Duncan's quiz and write the answers.**

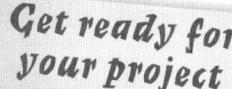

1 Who was George Washington? _____

2 Were the Wright brothers the inventors of the car? _____

3 Was Elvis Presley a famous jazz singer? _____

4 Who was the first person to walk on the moon? _____

5 Was William Shakespeare a writer? _____

6 Who were the New Orleans Rhythm Kings? _____

7 Who was Christopher Columbus? _____

8 Who were Greta Garbo and Marilyn Monroe? _____

24 **Choose famous people and research the facts for your quiz. Make notes.**

Prepare your project

1 _____

2 _____

3 _____

4 _____

5 _____

6 _____

25 **Write your quiz with the answers.**

Write your project in your notebook

Think!
- Use questions which start with *Who*, *Was* or *Were* in your quiz.

Writing Tip!
- Write the answers to your quiz on a separate page, slide or card!

Remember!
- Use *was* for one person.
- Use *were* for more than one person.

1 Who was …

Unit review and self-assessment

26 🔊 03:02 **Listen and number. Write the names of the professions.**

1 He's a _TV show host_ .

2 She's a _____ .

3 He's an _____ .

4 She's a _____ .

5 He's a _____ .

6 He's a _____ .

7 He's a _____ .

8 She's a _____ .

9 She's a _____ .

10 He's a _____ .

27 **Complete the sentences.**

1 Shakespeare _was a writer_ .

2 The Wright brothers _____ .

3 Louis Armstrong _____ .

4 Bill Haley and the Comets _____ .

5 Christopher Columbus _____ .

6 George Washington _____ .

7 The New Orleans Rhythm Kings _____ .

28 **Read and write questions and answers.**

Joseph
Character: happy, easy to please
Favorite food: apples

Sita
Character: quiet, shy
Favorite food: rice

1 (Joseph / naughty) *Was Joseph naughty?*
No, he wasn't. He was happy and easy to please.

2 (Sita's favorite food / pizza) _____

_____

3 (Sita / noisy) _____

_____

4 (Joseph's favorite food / bananas) _____

_____

29 **Read and write the answers. (See Student's Book page 40.)**

1 What's the capital of the US? _____

2 What's the population of the US? _____

3 How many states are there in the US? _____

4 What's the popular name for the US flag? _____

5 When was the Declaration of Independence? _____

6 What was George Washington's favorite food? _____

30 **Answer the questions. (See Student's Book page 42.)**

1 When was jazz music first popular?
Jazz music was first popular at the beginning of the 20th century.

2 What are country and western songs often about?

_____

3 What was rock 'n' roll originally from?

_____

4 What is rap music? _____

Assess your work in Unit 4.

Look and circle. ☺ ☺ ☺ ☹ ☹

Complete your *Progress Journal* for Unit 4.

5 🐾 Past times

Lesson 1

1 **Look and write.**

1. I look after my pet.

2. _____

3. _____

4. _____

5. _____

6. _____

2 ♻ **Order and write. Answer *Yes, I usually / sometimes do* or *No, I never do*.**

1. go / school / you / Do / bus / to / by / ?

   Do you go to school by bus? _____

2. have / Do / breakfast / for / cereal / you / ?

   _____ _____

3. you / sports / school / after / Do / play / ?

   _____ _____

4. read / you / sleep / Do / before / go / you / to / ?

   _____ _____

3 **Remember the quiz. (See Student's Book page 44.) Read and write the verbs.**

1. I go to school by car, but I ___walk___ to the park and the stores.

2. I usually _____ my grandparents on Sunday.

3. My teacher says that I sometimes _____ too much!

4. At home, I usually _____ hard when I do my homework.

5. At school, I sometimes _____ my snack with my friends.

Lesson 2

4 **Read and write correct sentences. (See Student's Book page 45.)**

1 Edinburgh Castle is on top of a high mountain.

No, it isn't. It's on top of a high rock.

2 Edinburgh Zoo is the only zoo in the UK with lions.

_____

3 Princes Street has many movie theaters.

_____

4 The Royal Yacht Britannia is a café.

_____

5 **Write sentences. Use these phrases. (See Student's Book page 45.)**

amazing view   beautiful gardens   long street   interesting museum

1 _At Edinburgh Castle, there's an amazing view._

2 _____

3 _____

4 _____

6 🔊 **Listen and complete. Write.**
03:07

		Where they want to go	Reason
Joseph		Princes Street	to see all the clothes stores
Sita			
Rosa			
Lisa			
And you?		I _____.	

Lesson 3

7 **Read the story and write the answers.**
(See Student's Book page 46.) 👥 **Ask and say.**

Picture 1: Who was Robert the Bruce? _He was King of Scotland._

Picture 2: Who defeated Robert the Bruce in six battles? _____

Picture 3: Why was Robert the Bruce disappointed? _____

Picture 4: Where did Robert the Bruce live? _____

Picture 5: How many times did the spider climb up the wall? _____

Picture 6: What did the spider start to do for the seventh time? _____

Picture 7: What did Robert the Bruce do? _____

Picture 8: How big was the Scottish army? _____

Picture 9: What did Edward II and the English army do? _____

8 **Write sentences about what happened in the story. Use the past tense verbs.**

1 (marched) _Edward I and the English army marched to Scotland._

2 (defeated) _____

3 (escaped) _____

4 (lived) _____

5 (watched) _____

6 (climbed) _____

9 **Read and circle. Write a review of the story. Tell your family about the story.**

1 The story is **a legend / an adventure story.**

2 The story is about how **Edward I defeated the French / Robert the Bruce defeated the English.**

3 Robert the Bruce failed in battle **four times / six times.**

4 He watched a spider make its web the **sixth / seventh** time.

5 In the seventh battle, **Edward II defeated the Scottish / Robert the Bruce defeated the English.**

6 At the end of the story, Scotland was **part of England / free.**

The story is a _____ about how
_____.

Robert the Bruce failed in battle _____.

He watched a spider make its web _____.

In the seventh battle, _____.

At the end of the story, Scotland was _____.

I think Robert the Bruce was _____
_____.

My favorite part of the story is when
_____.

I _____ this story. It's
_____.

Lesson 4

10 Read and write.

Greetings from Loch Ness

Dear Granny and Grandad,

Last Saturday, I (1) _____went_____ (go) to Loch Ness with some of my school friends. We (2) _____ (want) to see the famous monster, Nessie!

We (3) _____ (have) a picnic and (4) _____ (stay) all afternoon. We (5) _____ (talk) and (6) _____ (play) games. We also (7) _____ (listen) and (8) _____ (look) for Nessie, but we didn't notice anything strange in the lake :-(. Later we (9) _____ (visit) the Loch Ness museum and (10) _____ (watch) a movie about Nessie. We didn't believe a lot of the stories about Nessie, but we (11) _____ (laugh) a lot and (12) _____ (have) a great time.

Did you have a good weekend? I hope so!

Lots of love,
Duncan

11 Read and write. Be a grammar detective!

Past simple tense

- We use the past simple tense to talk about events in the past. All persons are the same.
- To make the past simple tense of regular verbs, we add *-ed* e.g. *look* → *looked*.
- For regular verbs that end in *e* we add *d* e.g. *live* → *lived*.
- For regular verbs that end in *y* we change *y* to *i* and and add *ed* e.g. *try* → *tried*.
- For some regular verbs that end in consonant, vowel, consonant, we double the final consonant e.g. *stop* → *stopped*.
- Some verbs are irregular and you need to learn these e.g. *go* → *went*, *have* → *had*.

Present	Past	Present	Past	Present	Past
jump	_jumped_	travel	_____	study	_____
like	_____	notice	_____	want	_____
hop	_____	close	_____	drop	_____

12 Read and write correct sentences. (See Activity 10.)

1 Duncan went to Loch Ness last Sunday.
   No, he didn't. He went to Loch Ness last Saturday.

2 Duncan wanted to see the lake.
   _____

3 Duncan watched a TV show.
   _____

4 Duncan visited the Loch Ness store.
   _____

5 Duncan had a boring time.
   _____

Lesson 5

13 Count the syllables. Write the sentences.
(See Student's Book page 49.) 🔊 Listen and check.
03:13

Four syllables
_____
_____

Five syllables
_____
_____

Six syllables
I walked along the path.
_____

Seven syllables
_____
_____

Eight syllables
_____
_____

14 Write questions and true answers about what you did yesterday.

1 _Did you listen to music?_ _____

2 _____ _____

3 _____ _____

4 _____ _____

5 _____ _____

15 🏠 Write five sentences about what you didn't do yesterday. Tell your family.

1 (play) _I didn't play_ _____

2 (go) _____

3 (have) _____

4 (watch) _____

5 (visit) _____

Lesson 6

16 **Read and answer the questions. (See Student's Book page 50.)**

1 What was a kilt originally? _It was a piece of cloth._

2 What is a sporran? _____

3 What did men use a kilt for at night? _____

4 What is the traditional cloth for kilts? _____

5 Who traditionally has their own tartan? _____

6 When do some men still wear kilts today? _____

17 🔊 03:16 **Listen and write.**

The Tiger Tracks SLN members tell Duncan their opinions about kilts.   POST ✓

Lisa	Steve	Rosa	Sita	Joseph
funny				

And you?   I _____.

Lesson 7
Everyday chit-chat

18 **Read and complete the dialogue in your own words.** 👥 **Act out.**

You: Guess what happened to me (1) _yesterday_?

Friend: What? Go on, tell me!

You: Well, I was (2) _____ and
(3) _____ walked by with
a (4) _____.

Friend: Did you say hello?

You: Yes, I did. She explained that
(5) _____.

Friend: What kind was it?

You: It was (6) _____.

History

Lesson 8

19 Look and write.
(See Student's
Book page 52).

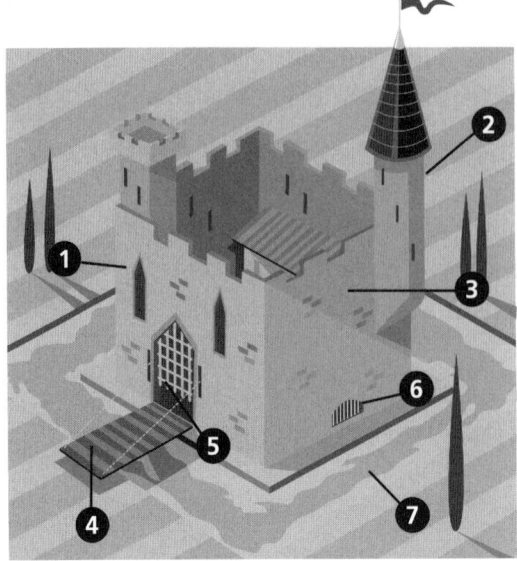

1 _____window_____
2 _____
3 _____
4 _____
5 _____
6 _____
7 _____

20 Read and write the answers. (See Student's Book page 52.)

1 How did people enter the castle?   _They entered the castle through a big gate._

2 Who lived in the castle?   _____

3 Who sometimes visited the castle?   _____

4 Where did servants prepare food?   _____

5 What did people drop in the moat?   _____

21 🔊 Listen and write.
03:21

Duncan is asking the Tiger Tracks SLN members their opinion about life in
a medieval castle.

	Opinion	Reason
Rosa	difficult	It was dark and cold.
Sita		
Steve		
Joseph		
Lisa		

22 🏠 Write your opinion about life in a medieval castle.
Tell your family.

My opinion

I think life in a medieval castle was _____ because

_____.

Project: My great-grandparents

23 Read Lisa's project. (See Student's Book page 53.) Write the
questions Lisa asked about her great-grandparents.

Get ready for your project

1  Did they have a car?

2 _____

3 _____

4 _____

5 _____

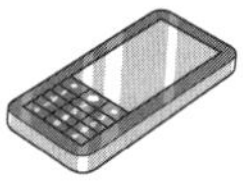

24 Write questions to ask about your great-grandparents.

Prepare your project

1 _____

2 _____

3 _____

4 _____

5 _____

25 Use the answers to write about life in the times of your great-grandparents.

Write your project in your notebook

Think!
- Write an introduction and a conclusion.

Writing Tip!
- Use *but* to contrast ideas.

Remember!
- Add *-ed* to regular verbs for affirmative sentences in the past.
- Use *didn't* (*did not*) for negative sentences in the past.
- Remember irregular verbs: *have* → *had*; *go* → *went*.

When they were young, my great-grandparents ...

_____

Unit review and self-assessment

26 🔊 **Listen and number. Write the sentences.**
03:23

1   _I watch TV._

2   _____

3   _____

4   _____

5   _____

6   _____

7   _____

8   _____

9   _____

10 _____

27 **Complete the postcard.**

> walk   have   ~~go~~   talk   stay   visit   watch   look   have   play

Dear Aunt Kay,

I hope you're well. Last Sunday I (1) ___went___ to Edinburgh Castle with Mom, Dad and my friend, Hamish. We (2) _____ up to the top of the castle and (3) _____ at the view. It was amazing! Afterwards we (4) _____ a picnic in the castle gardens. It was warm and sunny, and so we (5) _____ there all afternoon. Hamish and I (6) _____ and (7) _____ games. It was really fun. Later we (8) _____ the castle museum and (9) _____ a movie about life in medieval times. It was great and we (10) _____ a really good time!

Lots of love,

Duncan

28 Write questions and true answers about what you did last Saturday.

1 (soccer)   <u>Did you play soccer?</u>

_____

2 (movie   _____
theater)
              _____

3 (homework) _____

              _____

4 (music)   _____

              _____

5 (computer) _____

              _____

29 Read and write the answers. (See Student's Book page 50.)

1 What's the capital of Scotland?   _____

2 What's the official language of Scotland?   _____

3 What's the name of a famous Scottish cookie?   _____

4 Who was Robert Burns?   _____

5 How many islands are part of Scotland?   _____

6 What is the famous Scottish food 'haggis' made from? _____

30 Order the questions and write answers. (See Student's Book page 52.)

1 have / Did / dungeons / castles / medieval / ? <u>Did medieval castles have dungeons?</u>
<u>Yes,</u>_____

2 people / moat / Did / use / a / to / drawbridge / cross / the / ? _____

_____

3 medieval / live / Did / castles / animals / in / ? _____

_____

4 the / collect / people / trash / Did / ? _____

_____

Assess your work in Unit 5.

Look and circle.   😊   🙂   😐   🙁   ☹️

Complete your *Progress Journal* for Unit 5.

6 Fruit and vegetables

Lesson 1

1 **Read and write. Find the missing word.**

1 They're black or red and there are often two together.

2 They're green, red or purple.

3 They're small, sweet and red. They grow on a bush.

4 It's green or black and the same shape as a pear.

5 It's yellow and brown with green leaves at the top.

¹C H E R R I E S

2 **Write questions. Answer *Yes, I do* or *No, I don't*.**

1 Do you like carrots? _____

2 _____ _____

3 _____ _____

4 _____ _____

3 **Write about the fruit and vegetables.**

1 A cauliflower is white and has green leaves.

2 _____

3 _____

4 _____

Lesson 2

4 Classify the fruit and vegetables.
(See Student's Book page 55.)

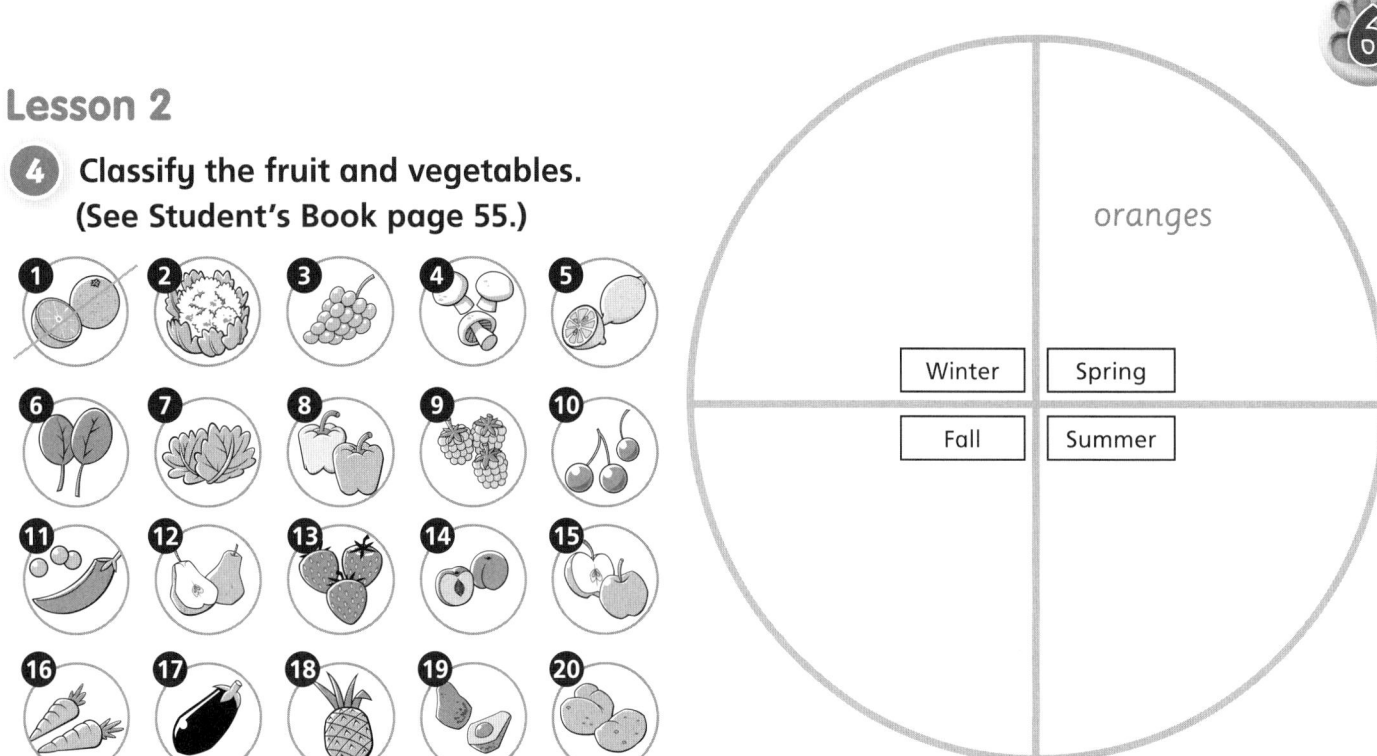

	Winter	Spring	oranges
	Fall	Summer	

5 Read and write correct sentences. (See Student's Book page 55.)

1 In South Africa spring is in December, January and February.

No, it isn't. Spring is in September, October and November.

2 In South Africa winter is in March, April and May.

_____

3 In South Africa fall is in June, July and August.

_____

4 In South Africa summer is in September, October and November.

_____

6 Listen and complete. Write.

03:28

TALK ABOUT IT!

	Sita	Rosa	Duncan	Lisa
When they want to visit South Africa	October			
Season	spring			
And you?	I _____.			

Lesson 3

7 **Read the story and write the answers.**
(See Student's Book page 56.) 🔲🔲 **Ask and say.**

Picture 1: What food is on the jetboat? _There are some sandwiches and fruit._____

Picture 2: What do they see above the river? _____

Picture 3: Where does the jetboat go? _____

Picture 4: What is in the water? _____

Picture 5: What do the children do? _____

Picture 6: Where is the crocodile? _____

Picture 7: How do the children feel? _____

Picture 8: What arrives in the sky? _____

Picture 9: What do they see from the helicopter? _____

8 **Answer the questions about Victoria Falls.**

1 What's the spray from the waterfall called?

_It's the 'smoke'._____

2 What's the noise of the waterfall called?

_____

3 What's the rainbow called?

_____

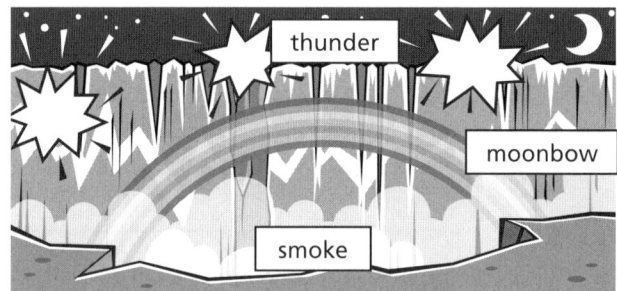

9 🏠 **Read and circle. Write a review of the story. Tell your family about the story.**

1 The story is **a travel story / an adventure story.**

2 The story is about **a vacation in South Africa / a school trip to Victoria Falls.**

3 The jetboat stops **on a rock / in the mud.**

4 There's a hungry **shark / crocodile** in the water.

5 They wait **three hours / four hours** for a rescue helicopter.

6 At the end of the story, they see **a rainbow / a 'moonbow'.**

The story is _____ about

_____.

The jetboat stops _____.

There's a _____ in the water.

They wait _____ for a rescue helicopter.

At the end of the story, _____.

I think the children in the story are

_____.

My favorite part of the story is when

_____.

I _____ this story. It's

_____.

Lesson 4

10 **Look and write sentences about small seeds.**

1 There are some small seeds inside lemons.

2 There aren't any _____

3 _____

4 _____

11 **Read and write a / an, some or any. Be a grammar detective!**

a / an, some and any
- We use *a* or *an* to talk about singular nouns we can count e.g. *a pit, an apple*.
- We use *some* for plural nouns we can count e.g. *some seeds, some cherries*.
- We also use *some* for nouns we can't count and which don't have plural forms e.g. *some food, some fruit, some smoke*. You can find examples in the story.
- We use *any* in negative sentences and questions.

1 There's ___a___ pineapple on the table.

2 There aren't _____ grapes on the table.

3 Is there _____ avocado on the table?
No, there isn't.

4 Are there _____ apples on the table?
Yes, there are.

5 There are _____ plates on the table.

12 **Look and write sentences.**

1 (apples)   There are some apples.

2 (cherries) _____

3 (pineapple) _____

4 (avocado)   _____

5 (bananas)   _____

Lesson 5

13 **Identify the word stress. Write the words.**
03:34 **(See Student's Book page 59.) Listen and check.**

Words with stress on first syllable

cherry _____ _____ _____

_____ _____ _____

_____ _____ _____

_____ _____ _____

14 **Write questions and answers about the picnic.**

1 Are there any plates?

   Yes, there are.

2 _____ _____

3 _____ _____

4 _____ _____

5 _____ _____

6 _____ _____

15 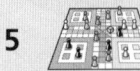 **Write true sentences about your classroom. Tell your family.**

1 There are some desks in my classroom. _____

2 _____

3 _____

4 _____

5 _____

Culture

Lesson 6

16 Read and answer the questions. (See Student's Book page 60.)

1 What's South Africa famous for? _It's famous for arts and crafts._

2 Where are the arts and crafts markets? _____

3 What can you learn about? _____

4 What are some sculptures made from? _____

5 What other stalls are there? _____

6 What can you find made from seasonal fruit and vegetables?

_____

17 🔊 **Listen and write.**
03:37

The Tiger Tracks SLN members tell Joseph what they want to look at in a South African arts and crafts market.

POST ✓

 Rosa	 Steve	 Lisa	 Sita	 Duncan
jewelry				

And you?   I _____.

Lesson 7
Everyday chit-chat

18 Read and complete the dialogue in your own words. 👥 Act out.

You: I love the market. This bakery is (1) _____my favorite_____ stall.

The (2) _____ look delicious.

Do you have (3) _____, please?

Man: Yes, we do. We have

(4) _____.

You: Can (5) _____, please?

Man: Yes, of course. Anything else for you?

You: Yes, please. Can (6) _____?

Man: OK. That's (7) _____.

CLIL · Science

Lesson 8

19 Complete the chart. (See Student's Book page 62.)

> cherries pumpkins eggplants cauliflowers strawberries pineapples
> mushrooms spinach lettuce lemons bananas plums ~~grapes~~ tomatoes peas

Red	Orange/Yellow	Green	Blue/Purple	White
			grapes	

20 Read and write the answers. (See Student's Book page 62.)

1 These keep you healthy and strong. _Green fruit and vegetables._

2 These are good for your heart and stomach. _____

3 These keep your eyes healthy. _____

4 These help your body absorb essential minerals. _____

5 These keep your heart healthy. _____

21 🔊 **Listen and write.**
03:42

Joseph is asking the Tiger Tracks SLN members about fruit and vegetables they eat.

	Color	Examples
Rosa	red	strawberries, red apples
Sita		
Steve		
Duncan		
Lisa		

22 🎓 **Write about you. Tell your family.** **My opinion**

I eat _____.

I like _____.

Project: My food diary

Get ready for your project

23 Read Duncan's project and complete his food diary.
(See Student's Book page 63.)

Monday

Breakfast orange juice and cereal   Break cookies and a banana
Lunch   meat, potatoes and peas   Snack sandwich and
Dinner   pizza with mushrooms   apple juice
            and red peppers

Tuesday

Breakfast _____   Break _____
Lunch   _____   Snack _____
Dinner   _____   _____
           _____

24 Complete your food diary.

Prepare your project

My food diary

Monday _____
_____
Tuesday _____
_____

25 Read your food diary and write a report.

Write your project in your notebook

Think!
- Write about each day and the food you had in order.

Writing Tip!
- Start each sentence: **On** for the day, **At** for *break*, **In** for *the afternoon*, **For** for meals.

Remember!
- Use the irregular past tense of *have: I had ...* to write your report.

On Monday I had ...

Unit review and self-assessment

26 🔊 **Listen and number. Write sentences.**

04:02

    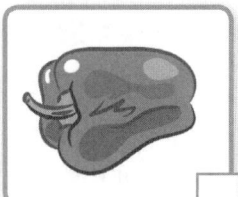

 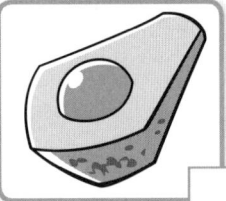 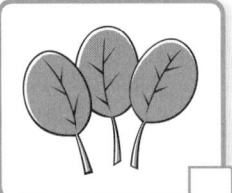  

1 _They're grapes._

2 _____

3 _____

4 _____

5 _____

6 _____

7 _____

8 _____

9 _____

10 _____

27 **Read and write *a*, *some* or *any*.**

Seeds or pits?

There are (1) __some__ small seeds inside grapes. But there aren't (2) _____ small seeds inside cherries. There's (3) _____ pit.

Are there (4) _____ small seeds inside strawberries? No, there aren't. But there are (5) _____ small seeds on the outside of strawberries!

Are there (6) _____ small seeds inside pineapples? Yes, there are. But there aren't usually (7) _____ small seeds inside the pineapples we buy in supermarkets.

28 Look and write questions and answers.

1 <u>Are there any avocados?</u>   <u>No, there aren't.</u>

2 _____   _____

3 _____   _____

4 _____   _____

5 _____   _____

29 Read and write the answers. (See Student's Book page 60.)

1 How many capital cities does South Africa have?   _____

2 What's the population of South Africa?   _____

3 How many official languages are there in South Africa?   _____

4 What's South Africa sometimes called?   _____

5 What's the name of a famous mountain in South Africa?   _____

6 What's South Africa number one in the world for?   _____

30 Read and write the missing words. (See Student's Book page 62.)

Fruit and vegetables contain many essential (1) n<u>utrients</u>   .

(2) V_____ and (3) m_____ can prevent

(4) d_____. (5) F_____ can prevent hunger and

help our digestion. (6) C_____ keeps our teeth and bones strong.

Assess your work in Unit 6.

Look and circle.   ☺   ☺   😐   ☹   ☹

Complete your Progress Journal for Unit 6.

7 Vacation in the city

Lesson 1

1 Read, match and write.

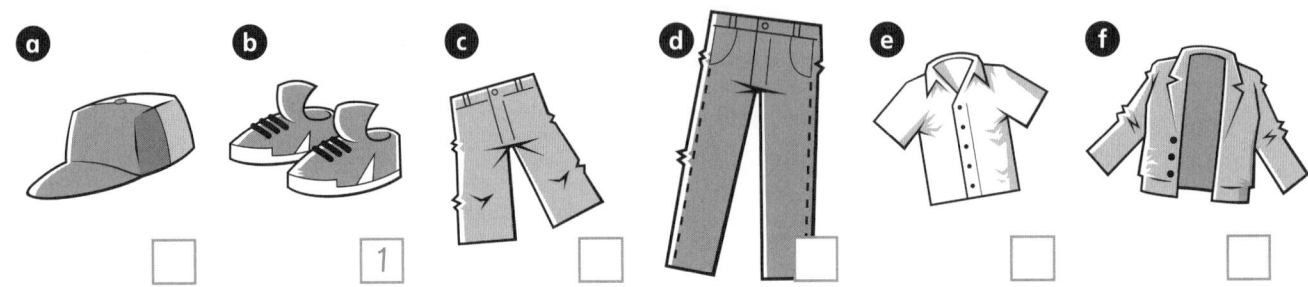

a b [1] c d e f

1 They're comfortable shoes for sports.	They're sneakers.
2 It's a type of hat. It's popular in summer.	
3 They aren't shorts, but they are short pants.	
4 It has a collar, buttons and short sleeves.	
5 They're blue denim pants. They're very popular.	
6 It's shorter than a coat and keeps you warm.	

2 Look and write questions and answers.

1 ✓ Are you taking a T-shirt?   Yes, I am.

2 ✗ _____   _____

3 ✓ _____   _____

4 ✗ _____   _____

3 Write about the clothes.

1 You wear a pullover to keep warm.

2 _____

3 _____

4 _____

❶ ❷ ❸ ❹

Lesson 2

4 **Read and write correct sentences. (See Student's Book page 65.)**

1 Gina's wearing sneakers. *No, she isn't. She's wearing sandals.*

2 Dave's wearing cropped pants. _____

3 Gina has a pullover. _____

4 Dave is wearing a pullover. _____

5 **Look and write.**

 Lizzie

 Paul

 Zara

1 *Lizzie's wearing* _____

She also has _____

2 *Paul* _____

_____

3 *Zara* _____

_____

6  **Listen and complete. Write.**
04:07

	Favorite clothes for fall
Duncan 🙂	jeans and a T-shirt
Rosa 🙂	
Steve 🙂	
Joseph 🙂	
And you?	My favorite _____.

Lesson 3

7 **Read the story and write the answers.**
(See Student's Book page 66). 🔁👥 **Ask and say.**

Picture 1: Where do Rosa, Joseph, Steve and Sita arrive? _They arrive at the hostel._

Picture 2: What does Sita want to see? _____

Picture 3: How is Rosa feeling? _____

Picture 4: Where do Rosa and Lisa go? _____

Picture 5: What does Rosa want to buy? _____

Picture 6: What do Duncan, Sita, Steve and Joseph decide to do? _____

Picture 7: Where do they all meet? _____

Picture 8: What's the present for Rosa? _____

Picture 9: What is in the hostel? _____

8 **Draw and write. Design a T-shirt for you and your friends.**

The T-shirt has a picture of _____

_____

_____

_____

_____

9 🎓 **Read and circle. Write a review of the story. Tell your family about the story.**

1 The story is **a photo story / a biography**.

2 The story is about **a pop star / a vacation in New York**.

3 Rosa's luggage wasn't on the **plane / train**.

4 Rosa buys a new **T-shirt / top**.

5 The present from the other children is **the same / different**.

6 At the end of the story, all the children wear the same **top / T-shirt**.

7 Rosa's **luggage / computer** is in the hostel.

The story is a _____ about

_____.

Rosa's luggage _____.

Rosa buys _____. The present from the other children _____.

At the end of the story, _____

_____.

Rosa's _____.

My favorite part of the story is when

_____.

I _____ this story. It's

_____.

Lesson 4

10 **Read and complete the dialogue.**

(1) <u>I want</u> to buy a shirt, please.

What kind of shirt (2) _____?

(3) _____ a short-sleeved shirt for summer.

They're here. (4) _____ to try one on?

Yes, (5) _____. Thank you.

What color (6) _____?

(7) _____ blue or green, please.

(8) _____ your friend want a shirt as well?

No, she (9) _____. She (10) _____ a jacket.

11 **Read and write. Be a grammar detective!**

Present simple review *want*

- We use nouns after *want* e.g. *I want a shirt.*
- We use verbs after *want to* e.g. *I want to go shopping.*
- We add *s* to for *he*, *she* and *it* e.g. *She wants a top. He wants to play.*
- The short form of *do not want* is *don't want*. The short form of *does not want* is *doesn't want*. We usually use the short form.

1 I <u>want</u> a cookie.

2 She _____ an apple.

3 He _____ to go to the movie theater.

4 _____ you _____ to go shopping? Yes, I _____.

5 _____ she _____ a new jacket? Yes, she _____.

6 _____ he _____ to go sightseeing? No, he _____.

12 **Look and write sentences.**

1 ✓ <u>She wants a jacket.</u>

2 ✓ _____

3 ✗ _____

4 ✓ _____

5 ✗ _____

6 ✗ _____

Lesson 5

13 🔊 **Listen and write. Identify the main sentence stress.**

04:13

1 _Does she want to go shopping?_

2 _____

3 _____

4 _____

5 _____

14 **Look and write questions and answers.**

1  _Does she want a cookie?_
   No, she doesn't.

2 _____
   _____

3 _____
   _____

4 _____
   _____

5 _____
   _____

6 _____
   _____

15 💬 **Write three sentences about what your friends want to do. Tell your family.**

1 _My friend wants to play_ _____

2 _____

3 _____

4 _____

Lesson 6

16 **Read and answer the questions. (See Student's Book page 70.)**

1 Where can you see wax figures?
At Madame Tussauds.

2 Where can you learn about flight simulators?
_____

3 Where can you see an exhibition of dinosaurs?
_____

4 Where can you learn about the birth of stars?
_____

5 Where can you see paintings?
_____

6 Where can you enjoy views of New York?
_____

17 🔊 **Listen and write where Lisa and her friends went.**
04:16

1 On Monday _they went to the New York Hall of Science_ .

2 On Tuesday _____.

3 On Thursday _____.

4 On Saturday _____.

Lesson 7

18 **Write about the Tiger Tracks SLN members' favorite places in New York. Answer the question. (See Student's Book page 71.)**

1 _Lisa's favorite place was the New York Hall of Science._

2 _____

3 _____

4 _____

5 Who didn't have a favorite place? _____ and _____

Lesson 8

19 Look and write the type of painting. (See Student's Book page 72.)

1 _____

2 _____

3 _____

20 Read and write the differences. (See Student's Book page 72.)

1 Some artists paint with oils.   <u>Some artists paint with watercolors.</u>

2 Some paintings are realistic.   _____

3 Some paintings are light.   _____

4 Some paintings are very big.   _____

21 Look and write about the painting. (See Student's Book page 72.)

1 In this painting, I can see <u>a woman and</u>

_____.

2 There is _____

_____.

3 There are _____

_____.

4 I think this painting is _____

_____.

22 Write about you. Tell your family.

My opinion

I **love** / **like** / **don't like** looking at paintings. I _____

_____

_____.

Project: A famous painting with people

Read Duncan's project and complete the notes. (See Student's Book page 73.)

Get ready for your project

Title of painting: _____

Name of artist: Augustus Leopold Egg   Date: _____

Scene of the painting: _____

People in the painting: _____

What the painting makes me feel: _____

Make notes to describe the painting you choose.

Prepare your project

Title of painting: _____

Name of artist: _____   Date: _____

Scene of the painting: _____

People/objects in the painting: _____

What the painting makes me feel: _____

Read your notes and write a description.

Think!
- Follow the order of your notes when you write your project.

Writing Tip!
- Use the phrase *It makes me feel …* to describe your personal response.

Write your project in your notebook

Remember!
- Use the past tense for the date of the painting.
- Use the present simple and present continuous to describe the painting and say your opinion.

The title of this painting is …

Unit review and self-assessment

26 🔊 **Listen and number. Write sentences.**
04:21

1				

1 _They're sandals._   6 _____

2 _____   7 _____

3 _____   8 _____

4 _____   9 _____

5 _____   10 _____

27 **Read and complete the dialogue.**

(1) _I want_ to buy a pullover, please.

What kind of pullover (2) _____ ?

(3) _____ a warm pullover to wear in winter.

They're here. (4) _____ to try one on?

Yes, (5) _____ . Thank you.

What color (6) _____ ?

(7) _____ red or black, please.

(8) _____ your friend want a pullover as well?

No, he (9) _____ . He (10) _____ a pair of jeans.

28 **Write questions and answers.**

1 _Does she want a banana?_ _____

_____

2 _____

_____

3 _____ _____

4 _____ _____

5 _____ _____

29 **Read and write correct sentences. (See Student's Book page 70.)**

1 The Top of the Rock has a five-level observation deck.

No, it doesn't. It has a three-level observation deck.

2 Madame Tussauds is a fashion museum.

_____

3 The Museum of Modern Art is a science museum.

_____

4 The exhibition of dinosaurs is at the Hayden Planetarium.

_____

5 You leave Earth at the New York Hall of Science.

_____

30 **Read and write the missing words. (See Student's Book page 72.)**

1 A painting of an individual person is a _portrait_ .

2 A painting of a view of a place is a _____.

3 A painting of objects, flowers, fruit or vegetables is a _____.

4 Paintings which show things as they are in real life are _____.

5 Paintings which show combinations of lines, shapes and colors are _____.

Assess your work in Unit 7.

Look and circle. 😊 🙂 😐 🙁 ☹️

Complete your *Progress Journal* for Unit 7.

🐾 Songs bank activities

Song 1: Let's communicate!

1 Look and write the words. 🔊 Listen and check (✓) the gadgets in the song.
04:29

1 ☐

computer

2 ☐

_____

3 ☐

_____

4 ☐

_____

5 ☐

_____

6 ✓

_____

7 ☐

_____

8 ☐

_____

2 Write the chorus. 🔊 Listen and check.
04:29

> Technology   communicate
> great   is   ~~Life~~   gadgets
> We
> have   is   fantastic   Let's

Life _____

_____

_____

_____

3 Write about your favorite gadget. Tell a friend.

> My favorite gadget is my mom's cell phone. It has a digital camera, an MP3 player and some great apps. It's very light and easy to use.

My favorite _____

_____

_____

_____

Look and circle: My American Tiger song score.

1   2   3   4   5   6   7   8   9   10

Reason: _____

Song 2: The Cool Crowd

1 Look, read and write. Listen and number the sentences in order.
04:31

A Some girls are  _____. ☐

B A boy is  _windsurfing_____ . 1

C A girl is  _____. ☐

D Some boys are  _____. ☐

2 Match and say the words that rhyme. Listen and check.
04:31

ocean   well   bright   brave

wave   shell   care

kite   hair   motion

3 Write sentences about the Cool Crowd.

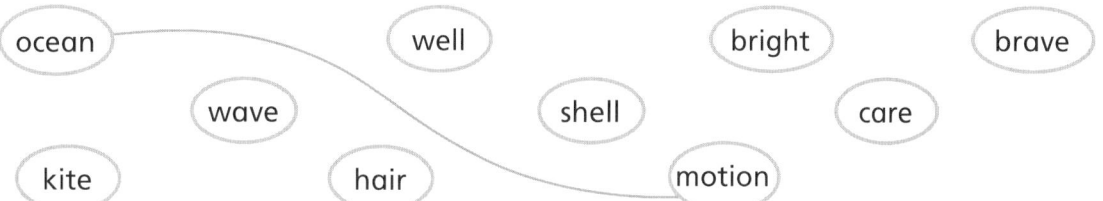

1 (play) _The Cool Crowd is playing in the ocean._
2 (ride) _A boy is_____
3 (move) _____
4 (look) _Some_____
5 (wear) _____

Look and circle: My American Tiger song score.

1   2   3   4   5   6   7   8   9   10

Reason: _____

Song 3: Red Alert!

1 Look and write the words. 🔊 04:33 Listen and check (✓) the animals in the song.

1 ✓ __elephant__   2 _____   3 _____   4 _____   5 _____

6 _____   7 _____   8 _____   9 _____   10 _____

Which two animals aren't in the song? The _____ and the _____.

2 Read and write. Number the sentences in the order of the song.
🔊 04:33 Listen and check.

Global warming   ~~Loss of habitat~~   Hunting and poaching   Pollution

A People cut down forests. ☐   _Loss of habitat_____

B The Earth is getting hotter. ☐   _____

C People hunting animals for their skins or horns. ☐   _____

D Trash in rivers you can see. ☐   _____

3 Draw and write. Make a 'Red Alert!' poster.

RED ALERT!
• Save endangered animals!
• Stop hunting rhinos for their horns!
• Never throw trash in rivers or the ocean!

Look and circle: My American Tiger song score.

1   2   3   4   5   6   7   8   9   10

Reason: _____

Song 4: Who was it?

1 **Read and write the answers.** 🔊 **Listen and check.**
04:35

Lucas ~~Gavin~~ Maya

1 Who talked to the movie star on the radio?

It was Gavin.

2 Who helped the chef in the burger bar?

_____

3 Who watched the inventor on the TV show?

_____

2 **Write a verse of the song. Draw a picture.** 🔊 **Listen and sing your verse.**
04:36

Who _____

_____?

Did you _____

_____?

Who me? Oh no! Not me!

I _____.

It _____!

3 **Write sentences about what you didn't do last weekend.**

1 (watch) I didn't watch TV.

2 (play) _____

3 (go) _____

4 (have) _____

5 (visit) _____

6 (listen) _____

Look and circle: My American Tiger song score.

1	2	3	4	5	6	7	8	9	10

Reason: _____

Song 5: The fruit and veg song

1 Listen and write the answers. 🔊 04:37 Listen again and check.

1 When do we eat fruit and vegetables? <u>In every season.</u>

2 What do fruit and vegetables have? _____

3 What colors are fruit and vegetables? _____

4 When do fruit and vegetables grow? _____

5 How do we eat fruit and vegetables? _____

6 What do they have that your body needs? _____

2 Complete the verse with the colors. 🔊 04:37 Listen and check.

Some fruit and veg are ____<u>red</u>____, some are _____ or _____.

Some fruit and veg are _____, some are _____, too.

Some fruit and veg are _____, and some are _____.

Fruit and veg keep you healthy, happy and bright.

3 Order and write your list of top six favorite fruit and vegtables. 👥 Tell a friend.

1 _____
2 _____
3 _____
4 _____
5 _____
6 _____

Look and circle: My American Tiger song score.

| 1 | 2 | 3 | 4 | 5 | 6 | 7 | 8 | 9 | 10 |

Reason: _____

Song 6: Tiger Tracks vacation song

1 🔊 **Listen and write sentences about what the characters want to do.**
04:39

1   *They want to look cool whatever the weather.*
2   *They* _____
3   _____
4   _____
5   _____

2 **Match and say the words that rhyme.** 🔊 **Listen and check.**
04:39

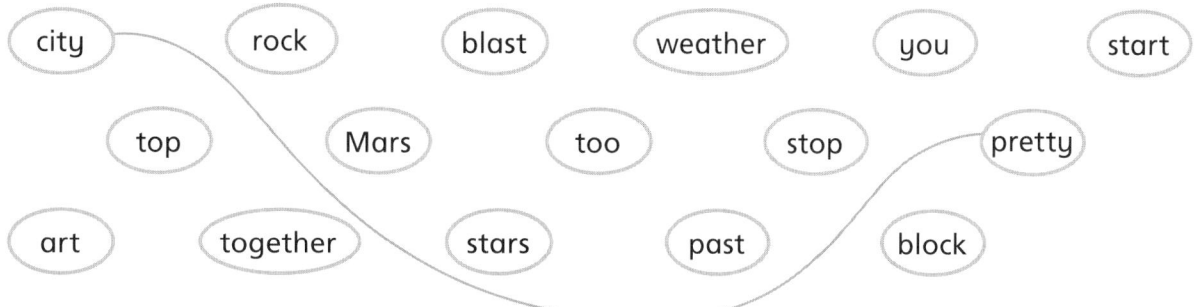

city   rock   blast   weather   you   start

top   Mars   too   stop   pretty

art   together   stars   past   block

3 **Write what you want to do on vacation.**
Talk to a friend. Write what they want to do.

I want to _____   My friend wants to _____

_____   _____

_____.   _____.

I _____   He /She _____

_____   _____

_____.   _____.

Look and circle: My American Tiger song score.

1   2   3   4   5   6   7   8   9   10

Reason: _____

79

Macmillan Education
4 Crinan Street
London N1 9XW
A division of Macmillan Publishers Limited

Companies and representatives throughout the world

ISBN 978-1-380-00499-4

Text © Carol Read and Mark Ormerod 2017
(Additional material by Katie Powell)
Design and illustration © Macmillan Publishers Limited 2017

The authors have asserted their right to be identified as the authors
of this work in accordance with the Copyright, Designs and Patents
Act 1988.

This edition published 2017
First edition entitled "Tiger Tracks" published 2013 by Macmillan
Publishers Limited
Previous edition entitled "Tiger Time" published 2015 by Macmillan
Publishers Limited

Original design by Blooberry Design Ltd
Original page make-up by Andrew Magee Design Ltd
This edition revised and updated by Composure
Illustrated by Vladimir Aleksic (Beehive), Humberto Blanco
(Sylvie Poggio), Ted Brandt (Bright Agency), Kevin Hopgood
(Beehive), Ann Kronheimer, Paul McCaffrey (Sylvie Poggio),
Andrew Painter, Andy Parker, Shahab Shamshirsaz (Sylvie
Poggio), Emma Shaw Smith (Sylvie Poggio),
Original cover design by Astwood Design Consultancy
This edition cover design revised and updated by Andrew Magee
Design Ltd
Cover photographs provided by Stockbyte/PunchStock, Getty
Images, Thinkstock, Corbis, DigitalStock/Corbis, Macmillan
Publishing Ltd/Stuart Cox

Authors' acknowledgments
We would like to thank everyone at Macmillan Education in the
UK and in Spain who has helped us in the development and the
production of these materials. We would also like to thank all the
teachers who have taken time to read, pilot and give feedback at
every stage of writing the course. Special thanks from Carol to Alan,
Jamie and Hannah for their encouragement and support. Special
thanks from Mark to Carlos for his patience and understanding.

The publishers would like to thank the following teachers:
Amparo Fernández Ortiz, CEIP La Patacona, Alboraya, Valencia;
Anna Esteban Nieto, Escola Jaume Ferran I Clua, Valldoreix,
Barcelona; Carlota López Petidier, CEIP Miguel de Cervantes,
Torrejón de Ardoz, Madrid; María del Mar Rodríguez Rodríguez,
Escola Els Pins, Barcelona; Mª Inmaculada Cercadillo Torrecilla,
CEIP Gabriel García Márquez, Getafe, Madrid; Paco Sansaloni Felis,
CEIP Cervantes, Gandía, Valencia; Patricia Meneses Dekker, Escola
Esteve Barrachina, Sitges, Barcelona; Teresa Rofes Bauzá, Escola
Barcelona, Barcelona.

The authors and publishers would like to thank the following for
permission to reproduce their photographs:
Alamy p9(tm), Alamy/Radius Images p19(tmrr), Alamy/David Lee
p61(cr), Alamy/John McKenna p50(tr), Alamy/louise murray p19(tr),
Alamy/Image Source Plus p19(tl), Alamy/Cre8tive Studios p78(cl),
Alamy/Art Directors&TRIP pp41(cr); **Bananastock** p9(cr);
The Bridgeman Art Library pp70, 71(cr); **Corbis**/Robert
Michael p19(tml), Corbis/MiguelCaibarién/Novarc p15(tl), Corbis/
Marsden,David/the food passionates p78(cmr), Corbis/Joe Stevens./
Retna Ltd p35(1), Corbis/Klaus Tiedge p38, Corbis/Hugh Sitton
p49(tr); **Digital Stock** p27(tr), 32(l), Digital Stock/Corbis p29; **The
Fitzwilliam Museum, Cambridge** p9(r); **Getty Images** pp25(tr),
Getty Images pp35(3), 40(tr), 45(2), Getty Images/Bloomberg p45(3),
Getty Images/Fazer44 p31(cr), Getty Images/Age footstock p3(tl),
Getty Images/Chris Hepburn p45(1), Getty Images/Stuart Pearce
p19(tmr), Getty Images/Maria Toutoudaki p39(tr), Getty Images/
WireImage p35(2); **Macmillan**/\David Tolley pp63; **Photodisc**
pp32(c); **Pixtal** p25(tl); **Rex** p45(4), REX/Charles Knight p59(tr), Rex/
Julian Makey p69(tr), REX/SIPA USA-KT/SIPA p35(4); **Shutterstock**/
Eremin Sergey p31(cr), Shutterstock/Anton_Ivanov p69(tr);
Superstock p42; **ThinkStock**/istockphoto pp27(cr), Thinkstock/
Photodisc p19(tmr), Thinkstock/ Pixland p11(cr). Commissioned
photography by Macmillan Publishers Ltd/ Stuart Cox

Author photograph (Carol Read) by Michael Selley

Printed and bound in Singapore

2021 2020 2019 2018
10 9 8 7 6 5 4 3 2